ISAAC ASIMOV'S NEW LIBRARY OF THE UNIVERSE

COSMIC DEBRIS:
THE ASTEROIDS

BY ISAAC ASIMOV
WITH REVISIONS AND UPDATING BY GREG WALZ-CHOJNACKI

Gareth Stevens Publishing
MILWAUKEE

For a free color catalog describing Gareth Stevens' list of high-quality books, call 1-800-542-2595 (USA) or 1-800-461-9120 (Canada). Gareth Stevens' Fax: (414) 225-0377.

Mr. Walz-Chojnacki would like to thank Drs. James Scotti and David Tholen for helpful discussion during the preparation of this edition.

Library of Congress Cataloging-in-Publication Data

Asimov, Isaac.
  Cosmic debris: the asteroids / by Isaac Asimov and Greg Walz-Chojnacki.
    p. cm. — (Isaac Asimov's New library of the universe)
  Rev. ed. of: The asteroids. 1988.
  Includes index.
  ISBN 0-8368-1130-5
  1. Asteroids—Juvenile literature. [1. Asteroids.]
 I. Walz-Chojnacki, Greg, 1954-. II. Asimov, Isaac. The asteroids.
 III. Title. IV. Series: Asimov, Isaac. New library of the universe.
 QB651.A84 1994
 523.4'4—dc20   94-15434

This edition first published in 1994 by
Gareth Stevens Publishing
1555 North RiverCenter Drive, Suite 201
Milwaukee, Wisconsin 53212, USA

Revised and updated edition © 1994 by Gareth Stevens, Inc. Original edition published in 1988 by Gareth Stevens, Inc., under the title *The Asteroids.* Text © 1994 by Nightfall, Inc. End matter and revisions © 1994 by Gareth Stevens, Inc.

Project editor: Barbara J. Behm
Design adaptation: Helene Feider
Editorial assistant: Diane Laska
Production director: Susan Ashley
Picture research: Kathy Keller
Artwork commissioning: Kathy Keller and Laurie Shock

Printed in the United States of America

1 2 3 4 5 6 7 8 9 99 98 97 96 95 94

To bring this classic of young people's information up to date, the editors at Gareth Stevens Publishing have selected two noted science authors, Greg Walz-Chojnacki and Francis Reddy. Walz-Chojnacki and Reddy coauthored the recent book *Celestial Delights: The Best Astronomical Events Through 2001.*

Walz-Chojnacki is also the author of the book *Comet: The Story Behind Halley's Comet* and various articles about the space program. He was an editor of *Odyssey*, an astronomy and space technology magazine for young people, for eleven years.

Reddy is the author of nine books, including *Halley's Comet, Children's Atlas of the Universe, Children's Atlas of Earth Through Time*, and *Children's Atlas of Native Americans*, plus numerous articles. He was an editor of *Astronomy* magazine for several years.

CONTENTS

We live in an enormously large place – the Universe. It's just in the last fifty-five years or so that we've found out how large it probably is. It's only natural that we would want to understand the place in which we live, so scientists have developed instruments – such as radio telescopes, satellites, probes, and many more – that have told us far more about the Universe than could possibly be imagined.

We have seen planets up close. We have learned about quasars and pulsars, black holes, and supernovas. We have gathered amazing data about how the Universe may have come into being and how it may end. Nothing could be more astonishing.

Most of the objects in the Universe are huge – planets, suns, galaxies. But there are small objects in space, as well. They would be too small to see if they were very far away from Earth, but some of them are right here, in our own Solar System. Just beyond the planet Mars, there are thousands of small bodies called asteroids. They come in a grand variety of shapes and sizes. Some come very close to us at times, and some are quite far away. Some orbit the Sun in peculiar paths. These asteroids may prove very important to us one day.

Isaac Asimov

To Be or Not To Be – A Planet?

When is a planet not a planet? – When it's an asteroid.

For example, Ceres is a body in space that was discovered in 1801 between the orbits of Mars and Jupiter. It is smaller than any planet – only about 600 miles (960 kilometers) across. During the following years, astronomers found still more planets in the same region, all of them even smaller than Ceres. These bodies seemed like a pile of rocks circling the Sun. Astronomers referred to them as minor planets and as *asteroids*, which means "starlike." Asteroids are so small that they seem to be just dots of light that look like stars, even through telescopes.

About ten thousand asteroids have been discovered to date, and there may be hundreds of thousands more to find.

Opposite: In this artist's rendition of the asteroids, our view is from just beyond Jupiter. Also clearly visible are Mars, which is just within the belt of asteroids, and Earth. Near the Sun, which glows faintly from about 500 million miles (800 million km) away, Venus and Mercury are just visible.

Inset: A portrait of the asteroid Ceres.

The Missing Planet?

Actually, astronomers of days gone by were looking for these asteroids, even though they may not have known it. That is, one astronomer had noticed that most planets in the Solar System seemed to be spaced in a regular pattern. But the space between Mars and Jupiter didn't fit the pattern. The large space between these planets led astronomers to believe there might be another planet in between them. The planet would have to be a small one, or else it would already have been discovered. When Ceres was found, astronomers thought it was the missing planet. But the real surprise came when they found not one, but thousands of planets in the space between Mars and Jupiter! This space is called the asteroid belt.

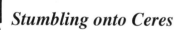

Stumbling onto Ceres

Almost two hundred years ago, a group of German astronomers planned to search the heavens for a possible planet between Mars and Jupiter. They carefully divided sections of the sky among themselves. Then, just before they were ready to start, word came that an Italian astronomer, Giuseppe Piazzi, who wasn't looking for a new planet at all, happened to stumble onto Ceres while he was watching for other objects. He discovered Ceres on January 1, 1801.

Above and right: These illustrations clearly show the position of the asteroid belt between Jupiter and Mars. Also shown are two clumps of asteroids, the so-called Trojan asteroids, in the orbit of Jupiter that lead and trail the planet in its journey around the Sun. These diagrams are not drawn to scale. The Sun, for instance, is actually more than one hundred times larger than Earth.

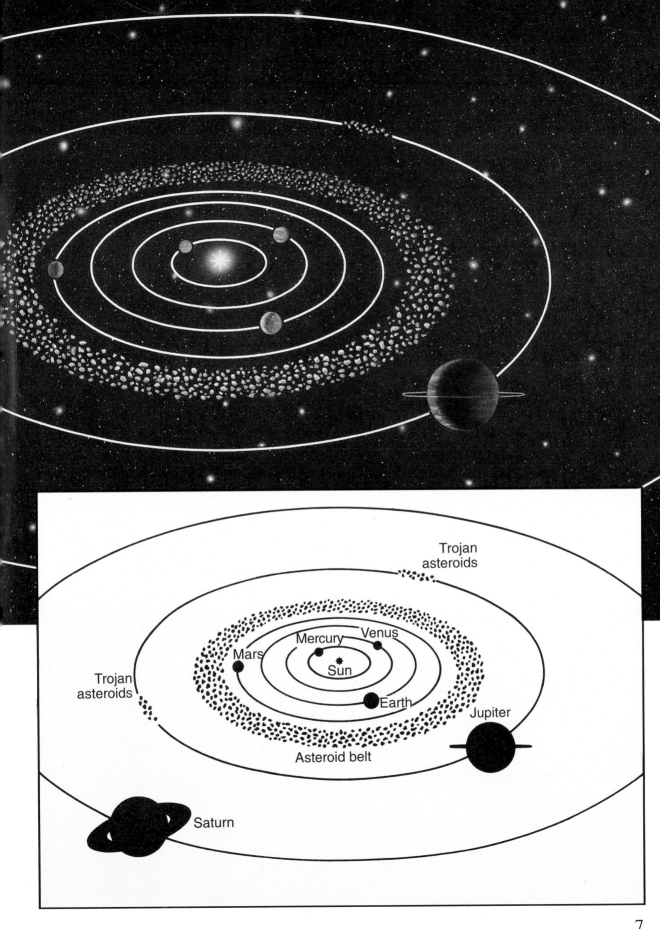

Trojan
asteroids

Mercury Venus

Mars

Sun

Earth

Trojan
asteroids

Jupiter

Asteroid belt

Saturn

The Many Sizes and Shapes of Asteroids

No asteroid has ever been discovered that is larger than Ceres, but there must be dozens that are more than 100 miles (160 km) across. Most asteroids, however, are only a few miles across. Some are dark, and some are very bright. One of the earliest asteroids discovered was Vesta. Vesta reflects so much light it can sometimes just barely be seen. Small asteroids are usually brick shaped. One asteroid, called Hector, is in the shape of a dumbbell. But perhaps it's really two asteroids stuck together. Only the largest asteroids look round.

Opposite: Is Hector a single dumbbell-shaped asteroid or two asteroids stuck together?

Inset: A portrait of Vesta, one of the brightest asteroids in the sky (the larger, round, bright object in the center of the photo). Only the fourth asteroid to be discovered – after Ceres, Pallas, and Juno – Vesta was first spotted and identified in 1807. It would be another forty years before the discovery of any more asteroids.

! Naming the asteroids – by the thousands!

At first, asteroids were named after goddesses such as Ceres, Pallas, Vesta, Juno, and so on. However, when great numbers of asteroids were discovered, it became difficult to name them all. They began to be named for astronomers, for other famous people, for friends, for cities, for colleges, and so on. From the beginning, most of the names were feminine, such as Washingtonia and Rockefellia. But the thousandth was named Piazzi after the man who discovered the first asteroid. One asteroid was originally named Drake, but to make it different, perhaps more feminine, it was spelled backward as Ekard.

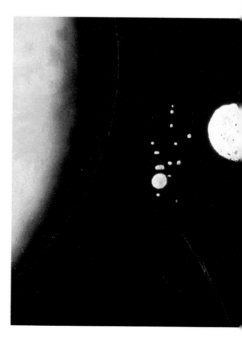

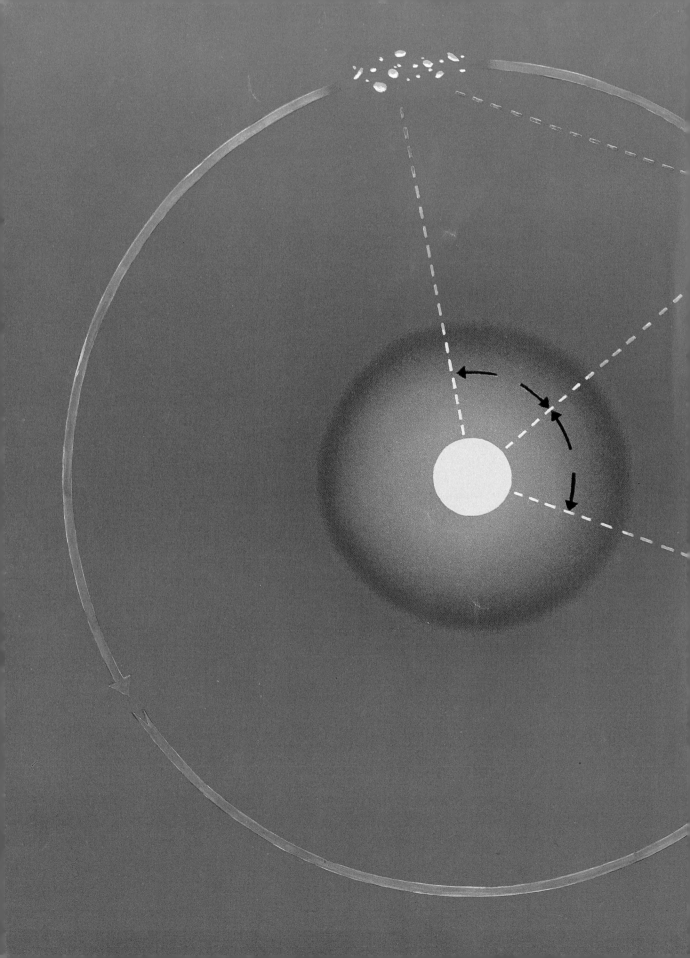

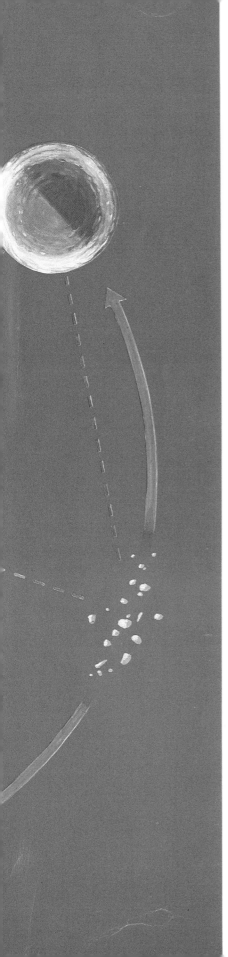

Jupiter's Captured Moons

Jupiter, the huge planet at the outer edge of the asteroid belt, has captured many asteroids. It has eight small moons circling it, and all of them are probably captured asteroids. There are also a number of asteroids that follow Jupiter in its orbit, and others that move ahead of it in its orbit. If you draw a line from Jupiter to each group of asteroids, and then draw lines from Jupiter and both groups to the Sun, you will have two equal-sided triangles. These groups are named *Trojans* after heroes in the ancient Greek tales of the Trojan War.

Left: Jupiter and the Trojan asteroids in orbit. In their trek around the Sun, Jupiter and its army of asteroids hold to a steady formation.

Below: A close-up view of one of Jupiter's Trojan asteroids.

Top: The asteroid Hidalgo *(right)* seems to dwarf Jupiter as it approaches the planet in the far reaches of our Solar System beyond the asteroid belt.

Bottom: A portrait of Pluto and Charon. What is the real nature of their relationship – a planet and its satellite? a double planet? or a pair of revolving asteroids?

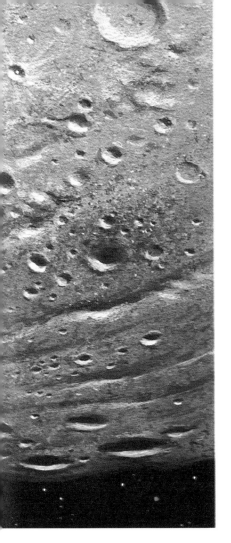

Beyond the Asteroid Belt

A few asteroids lie far beyond the asteroid belt — beyond even Jupiter and its faithful family of asteroids. The asteroid Hidalgo swoops out nearly to Saturn, and another, Chiron, moves in the space between Saturn and Uranus. Astronomers think Saturn's outermost moon, Phoebe, may be a captured asteroid. And Neptune's outer moon, Nereid, may be one, too. Some astronomers even think the farthest planet, Pluto, and its moon, Charon, are so small that they should be considered asteroids. In the last few years, astronomers have begun to find objects beyond the orbit of Neptune. They think there may be a huge number of asteroids in a new belt beyond the known planets.

? *Sizing up Ceres — big asteroid or little planet?*

When Ceres was first discovered, everyone was surprised at how small it was. It is only 600 miles (960 km) across, about the width of France; while Mercury, the smallest planet after Pluto, is over 3,000 miles (4,800 km) across, about the width of North America. However, when the other asteroids were discovered, astronomers were surprised at how big Ceres was in comparison. It was twice the diameter as any other asteroid. It had five times the mass as any other asteroid. In fact, some astronomers calculate that Ceres has one-tenth as much mass as all the other asteroids put together. Why is it so large? Scientists do not know.

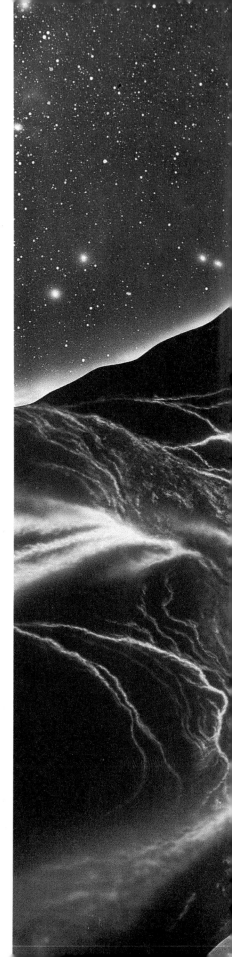

Asteroids or Comets?

We know that most asteroids are found between Mars and Jupiter, while others lie even farther out. But not all asteroids behave in the same way. A few have long, thin orbits that take them much closer to the Sun than others. Such orbits resemble the orbits of some comets. Recently, astronomers have carefully studied the light from some of these asteroids and have found that they look more like comets than asteroids. Astronomers suspect that many bodies traveling near the Sun, that are thought to be asteroids, aren't asteroids at all. Instead, they may actually be old comets that no longer glow like ordinary comets.

? The shiniest asteroid – but why?

The brightest asteroid is Vesta. It is the third largest asteroid, at 300 miles (480 km) across, but only half the size of Ceres. However, Vesta reflects much more light than Ceres. In fact, if you know exactly where to look and have very sharp eyes, you can see Vesta without a telescope. Yet it was only the fourth asteroid to be found. Scientists do not know why Vesta is so shiny. It may be covered with ice, but why should it be covered with ice when Ceres isn't?

Right: Its glow mostly gone, an old comet nucleus keeps its appointment with the Sun.

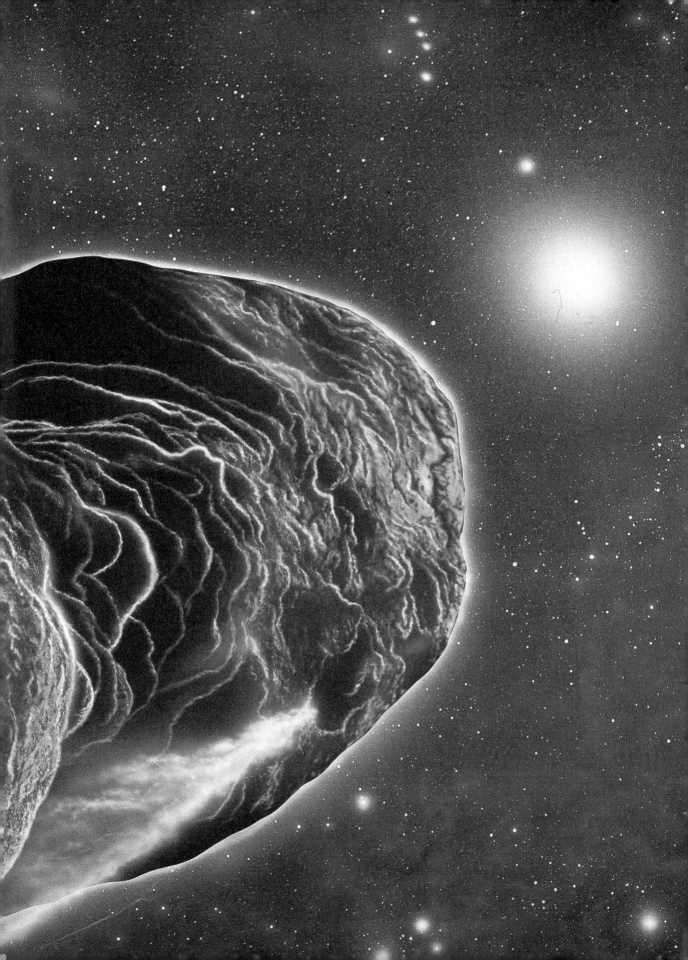

Asteroids – A Threat to Earth?

For a long time, astronomers thought of asteroids as members of the outer Solar System, beyond Mars. In 1932, though, an asteroid named Amor was discovered. This object had an orbit that took it between the asteroid belt and Earth. And in 1937, a small asteroid named Hermes passed within 488,000 miles (785,000 km) of Earth. Suddenly, scientists realized asteroids were a possible threat to our planet.

More recently, astronomers have been finding dozens of asteroids that travel in orbits close to Earth. And it's now known that, several times a year, small, rocky asteroids even occasionally strike Earth or explode in Earth's atmosphere.

Some asteroids, usually those containing a lot of metal, actually strike Earth. Usually only small ones do, and no great harm is done. However, in Arizona, there is a crater 3/4 mile (1.2 km) across where an asteroid struck fifty thousand years ago. We also know that craters on other planets were caused by crashing asteroids.

Top: A remarkable event in 1972 captured in a remarkable photo. Having entered Earth's atmosphere over Idaho, an asteroid – now a streaking meteor – flies above Jackson Lake, Wyoming. Astronomers believe it was 262 feet (80 m) in diameter, moved at an average speed of 33,000 miles (53,000 km) per hour, and weighed a million tons.

Opposite, bottom: The asteroid, Apollo, a scant 2 miles (3 km) in diameter, comes close to Earth's atmosphere. Just about every asteroid that comes close to Earth is quite small.

Left: A photo of the Leonid meteor shower streaking across Earth's atmosphere. The Leonid shower occurs every year, but it is exceptionally heavy every thirty-three years. The latest heavy shower was in 1966, so the next one will occur in 1999.

Picture Perfect

Our first hints of what asteroids might look like came when the *Viking* probes got a good view of the moons of Mars – Phobos and Deimos. These moons are dark, lumpy objects that fit the same profile astronomers had of asteroids.

In the 1990s, the *Galileo* probe looped through the asteroid belt twice on its way toward Jupiter. The probe traveled close to two asteroids, Gaspra and Ida, and snapped our first clear pictures of true asteroids. Other probes are planned that will come even closer to the other asteroids – and even go into orbit around them!

Opposite: This composite picture shows two moons and an asteroid – but they look similar to one another. The *upper* object is the asteroid Gaspra, which lies between Mars and Jupiter. Gaspra's picture was taken by the *Galileo* spacecraft in 1991. The two *lower* objects are Phobos *(left)* and Deimos *(right)*, the moons of Mars. Their pictures were taken by the *Viking* spacecraft in 1976. Astronomers suspect that Mars's moons are really asteroids that wandered too close to Mars and were captured by the planet's gravity.

Below: This photo shows the asteroid Ida, which was visited by *Galileo* in 1993. This asteroid looks like a long, lumpy potato. Only very large objects have enough gravity to pull rock into a round shape. Most asteroids are too small for that.

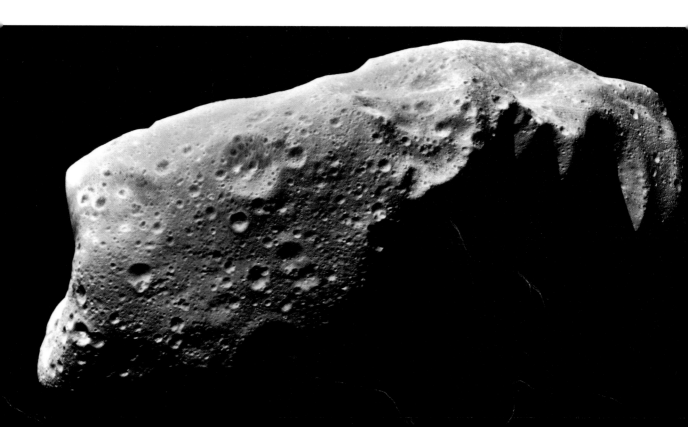

Space Mining

Asteroids that are just a few feet or meters across are called meteoroids. We see them as meteors when they enter Earth's atmosphere. If they strike Earth (as meteorites), they may even be useful to us on Earth. About one-tenth of the asteroids that strike Earth are almost pure nickel-iron. Thousands of years ago before humans learned how to get iron from ores, meteorites were the only supply of iron. Iron was valuable for making tools.

Even today, humans are mining metals made available by asteroids. The Sudbury Basin in Canada is known for its nickel and iron deposits. A look from space shows that those deposits lie in a crater left by an asteroid that smacked into our planet millions of years ago. The asteroid didn't actually bring the nickel and iron deposits found, but it may have helped the deposits form.

Opposite: There are asteroids whose orbits are similar to Earth's. These asteroids could be captured and towed back to Earth by "space tugs" for mining.

Bottom: Two views of humans working with asteroids. *(Left)* A prehistoric man examines a meteorite, looking for iron. *(Right)* An astronaut mines an asteroid in space in future times.

Journey to the Asteroids

Some day, after humans have established a base on Mars, they may venture farther outward. With Mars as a base, rocket probes may be sent to various asteroids. Perhaps even astronauts could visit asteroids. Ceres is quite far from the Sun, and this asteroid would be a very useful world on which to set up telescopes and other instruments to study stars and distant planets. Also, analyzing asteroids and finding out what elements they are made of could give us information about the early days of our Solar System.

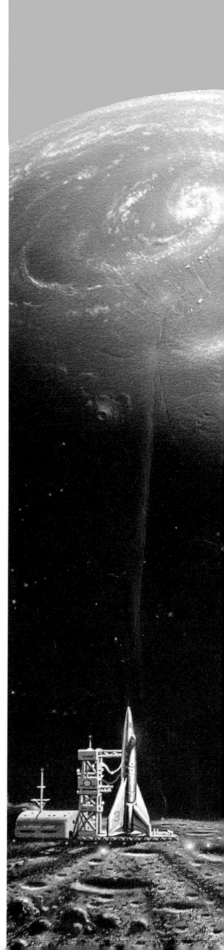

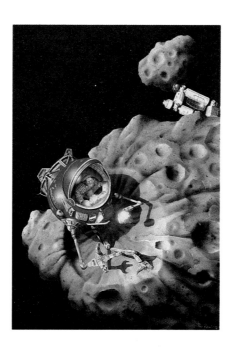

Opposite: A view of an Earthlike Mars from a base on one of Mars's moons. Future technology might make it possible to terraform Mars (make it like Earth). New gases could be put into Mars's atmosphere, thereby trapping sunlight and making the atmosphere like Earth's. Will Mars then become our springboard to the asteroids and beyond?

Right: An illustration of a miner taking samples from an asteroid. Note the movable arms on the craft and the homeship in the background.

Future Resources

Asteroids might become humanity's new mines in centuries to come. There must be tens of thousands of asteroids that are made of iron. They could supply us with all the iron and steel we could ever want. In addition, some asteroids are rocky and might serve as sources for other metals, and for oxygen, glass, concrete, and soil. Some are icy and might give us supplies of hydrogen, carbon, and nitrogen. These elements are not easy to obtain outside Earth, and they are very necessary to humans in space. Some asteroids might even be hollowed out and made into space stations where people could live and work.

Opposite, top, left: In future times, could diamonds be mined from asteroids? It's quite possible, since asteroids contain carbon, the material from which diamonds are made. Here a team of miners examines its find as machines called mass drivers transport both mined materials and entire asteroids back to a base.

Top, right: An assortment of machinery at work in an asteroid-gathering mission. This artist's conception is based on an actual NASA study of the technology that would be needed to put an asteroid into permanent orbit around Earth.

Left: In this artwork, a team of asteroid explorers is greeted by a geyser. The matter shooting upward was once part of a comet that slammed into this otherwise desolate asteroid.

? *The asteroids – a jigsaw planet?*

Why are some asteroids made of iron, some of rock, and some of icy materials? If a planet like Earth broke up, pieces of its center would be iron, pieces of its surface would be icy, and pieces from in between would be rocky. Was there once a large planet between Mars and Jupiter that broke up? Maybe, but all the asteroids together would compose only a very small planet, and astronomers think it was too small to break up if it existed. Maybe there wasn't a planet there after all. But why, then, are there different kinds of asteroids? Scientists do not know.

Science fiction or science fact?
A hollowed-out asteroid, now
a fully equipped spaceship,
cruises past Jupiter on its way
to the cosmos. Can you
imagine people being born,
growing up, raising families,
and spending their entire lives
as "space people" in ships like
this? One day, it could happen.

A New Frontier

Once there are people living on asteroids, these
asteroids will serve as starting points for more
space exploration. People from the asteroids
could build rockets to take them to the moons of
Jupiter and Saturn – and even farther. They
might explore the entire Solar System. Perhaps
some asteroids will be converted into huge
starships, and thousands of people on them will
drift outward, away from the Sun forever, on a
long, long journey to the distant stars. Who
knows? The asteroids might play an important
role as human beings start to colonize the
Galaxy – and begin their quest for other forms
of intelligent life.

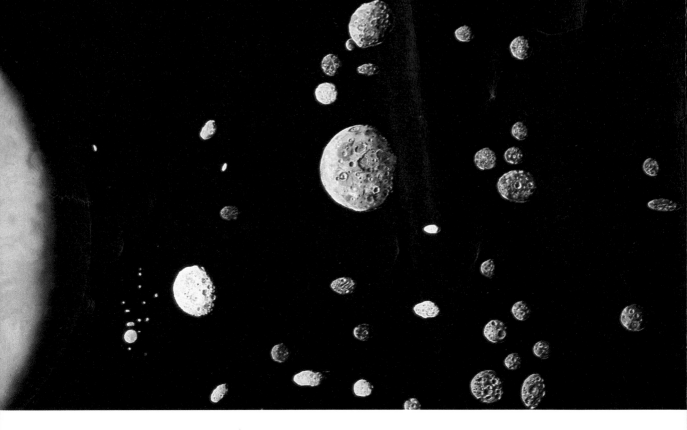

Record Set	Asteroid	Comments
Largest asteroid	Ceres	Diameter: 623-646 miles (1,003-1,040 km)
Smallest known asteroid	Hathor	Diameter: about 3/10 mile (0.5 km)
Brightest asteroid	Vesta	Only member of asteroid belt visible to naked eye
Darkest asteroid	Arethusa	Blacker than a blackboard
Shortest known rotation (spinning) period	Icarus	2 hours, 16 minutes
Longest known rotation	Glauke	1,500 hours
First asteroid to be discovered	Ceres	January 1, 1801
First asteroid to be discovered photographically	Brucia	December 20, 1891
Shortest time to revolve around Sun	Ra-Shalom	283 days (orbit is well within that of Earth)
Longest time to revolve around Sun	Hidalgo	Over 14 years (orbit is slightly beyond that of Saturn)*
First asteroid known to have a satellite	Herculina	Asteroid with diameter of 135 miles (217 km) was found to have a satellite with a diameter of 31 miles (50 km)
First masculine name for an asteroid	Eros	1898

* In 1977, an unusual object called Chiron was discovered. Its path is mostly between Saturn and Uranus, and it takes 50-68 years to orbit the Sun. For now, it has been designated as asteroidal, but it is no ordinary asteroid. Astronomers feel it may be a planetesimal *(see Glossary)* or even an escaped satellite of Saturn, and its statistics are not included in the record "bests" given on these pages.

Fact File: The Asteroids ✓

Opposite, top: An illustration, done to scale, of an assortment of asteroids – including all thirty-three known asteroids with diameters of 125 miles (200 km) or more. All asteroids are sized in proportion to one another and to the edge of Mars on the *left*. The black-and-white drawing at the bottom of this page is a guide to the names of each of the large asteroids, as well as to the Flora/Flores family of asteroids, all with diameters greater than 9.5 miles (15 km).

Opposite, bottom: Some "firsts" and "bests" of the asteroids. Keep in mind that new asteroids are being discovered all the time, and that records are made to be broken – even astronomical ones.

There are thousands upon thousands of them, and they come in a variety of sizes and shapes. They look like bricks, dumbbells, mountains, cosmic sausages, and even the island of Manhattan! They are named Iris, Flora, Davida, Cincinnati, Marilyn, Russia, and Claudia. One is even called Photographica, in honor of photography – at one time a brand-new way to discover asteroids in space.

We call them planetoids, minor planets, and occasionally, when they stray from their orbits, meteoroids. They are the asteroids.

Key

1	Pallas	20	Vesta
2	Winchester	21	Eugenia
3	Euphrosyne	22	Diotima
4	Bamberga	23	Psyche
5	Daphne	24	Lorely
6	Hector	25	Cybele
7	Juno	26	Thisbe
8	Eros	27	Europa
9	Iris	28	Flora/Flores
10	Ceres	29	Egeria
11	Bettina	30	Ursula
12	Nysa	31	Alauda
13	Patientia	32	Hebe
14	Themis	33	Eunomia
15	Hermione	34	Herculina
16	Fortuna	35	Interamnia
17	Hygiea	36	Davida
18	Camilla	37	Siegena
19	Dembowska		

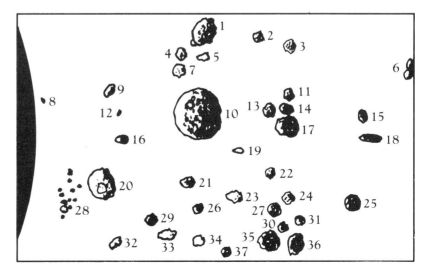

More Books about Asteroids

Comets and Meteors. Asimov (Gareth Stevens)
Comets and Meteors. Couper (Franklin Watts)
Comets and Meteors. Fichter (Franklin Watts)
Death from Space: What Killed the Dinosaurs? Asimov (Gareth Stevens)
Our Planetary System. Asimov (Gareth Stevens)
Sun, Moon and Planets. Myring (Usborne-Hayes)

Video

The Asteroids. (Gareth Stevens)

Places to Visit

You can explore the asteroid belt and other places in the Universe without leaving Earth. Here are some museums and centers where you can find a variety of space exhibits.

Air and Space Museum
Smithsonian Institution
601 Independence Avenue SW
Washington, D.C. 20560

Astrocentre
Royal Ontario Museum
100 Queen's Park
Toronto, Ontario M5S 2C6

Sydney Observatory
Observatory Hill
Sydney NSW 2000 Australia

Henry Crown Science Center
Museum of Science and Industry
57th Street and Lake Shore Drive
Chicago, IL 60637

NASA Lewis Research Center
Educational Services Office
21000 Brookpark Road
Cleveland, OH 44135

Edmonton Space and Science Centre
11211 - 142nd Street
Edmonton, Alberta K5M 4A1

Places to Write

Here are some places you can write for more information about asteroids. Be sure to state what kind of information you would like. Include your full name and address so they can write back to you.

National Space Society
922 Pennsylvania Avenue SE
Washington, D.C. 20003

Department of Industry
235 Queen Street
Ottawa, Ontario
K1A 0H5

Anglo-Australian Observatory
P. O. Box 296
Epping, NSW 2121 Australia

Jet Propulsion Laboratory
Public Affairs 180-201
4800 Oak Grove Drive
Pasadena, CA 91109

Glossary

asteroid: "starlike." The asteroids are very small "planets" made of rock or metal. There are thousands of them in our Solar System, and they mainly orbit the Sun in large numbers between Mars and Jupiter. But some show up elsewhere in the Solar System – some as meteoroids and some possibly as "captured" moons of planets such as Mars.

asteroid belt: the space between Mars and Jupiter that contains thousands of asteroids.

billion: the number represented by 1 followed by nine zeroes – 1,000,000,000. In some countries, this number is called "a thousand million." In these countries, one billion would then be represented by 1 followed by twelve zeroes – 1,000,000,000,000: a million million.

Ceres: the first asteroid to be discovered (1801).

Chiron: an unusual asteroidal body whose path is usually between Saturn and Uranus. Astronomers think its diameter may be as large as 404 miles (650 km), but they are not sure. They think Chiron may be a huge planetesimal or even an escaped moon of Saturn.

galaxies: the numerous large groupings of stars, gas, and dust that exist in the Universe. Our Galaxy is known as the Milky Way.

Hector: an unusual asteroid that seems to be shaped like a dumbbell.

meteor: a meteoroid that has entered Earth's atmosphere. Also, the bright streak of light made as the meteoroid enters or moves through the atmosphere.

meteorite: a meteoroid when it hits Earth.

meteoroid: a lump of rock or metal drifting through space. Meteoroids can be as big as asteroids or as small as specks of dust.

NASA: the space agency in the United States – the National Aeronautics and Space Administration.

Piazzi, Giuseppe: the Italian astronomer who discovered Ceres, the first asteroid to be named.

planetesimals: small bits of matter that, when joined together, may have formed planets.

planetoid: another name for an asteroid. In a way, this is a more accurate name, since the asteroids, or minor planets, are more "planetlike" than they are "starlike."

Pluto: the farthest planet in our Solar System and one so small that some astronomers believe it actually to be a large asteroid.

Solar System: our Planetary System – the Sun with the planets and all other bodies that orbit the Sun.

terraform: to make a body in space suitable for human life.

trapped asteroids: asteroids that are captured by the gravity of planets. The moons of certain planets are, in reality, trapped asteroids.

Universe: everything that we know exists and that we believe may exist.

Vesta: the brightest asteroid. It has a diameter of about 300 miles (480 km).

Index

Born in 1920, Isaac Asimov came to the United States as a young boy from his native Russia. As a young man, he was a student of biochemistry. In time, he became one of the most productive writers the world has ever known. His books cover a spectrum of topics, including science, history, language theory, fantasy, and science fiction. His brilliant imagination gained him the respect and admiration of adults and children alike. Sadly, Isaac Asimov died shortly after the publication of the first edition of *Isaac Asimov's Library of the Universe.*

The publishers wish to thank the following for permission to reproduce copyright material: front cover, © MariLynn Flynn 1986; 4, © William K. Hartmann; 4-5, © David Hardy; 6-7, 7, © Lynette Cook 1988; 8-9, © Andrew Chaikin; 9, © Julian Baum 1988; 10-11, © Sally Bensusen 1988; 11, © William K. Hartmann; 12-13 (both), © David Hardy; 14-15, © Julian Baum 1988; 16, © David Hardy; 16-17 (upper), © James M. Baker; 16-17 (lower), © David Milon; 18, 19, NASA/JPL; 20-21, © David Hardy 1987; 21 (upper), © William K. Hartmann; 21 (lower), © David Hardy 1987; 22, © Lamar Savings, Austin, Texas, by Pat Rawlings; 22-23, © David Hardy; 24, © Mark Maxwell 1988; 24-25 (upper), NASA; 24-25 (lower), © Kurt Burmann 1988; 26-27, © David Hardy 1987; 28, © Andrew Chaikin.